THE POP SINGER'S WARM-UP KIT

by LIS LEWIS

Because Stardom Takes Practice

The male vocal was sung by Scott Houghton; the female vocal was sung by Lis Lewis.
The audio was recorded by Keith Sterling at Straylight in Glendale, California.

PLAYBACK+
Speed • Pitch • Balance • Loop

To access audio, visit:
www.halleonard.com/mylibrary

7995-8707-8815-2125

ISBN 978-0-634-04297-3

CREATIVE CONCEPTS PUBLISHING

EXCLUSIVELY DISTRIBUTED BY
HAL•LEONARD®

Copyright © 2003 by HAL LEONARD CORPORATION
International Copyright Secured   All Rights Reserved

Visit Hal Leonard Online at
www.halleonard.com
www.TheSingersWorkshop.com

Contact us:
Hal Leonard
7777 West Bluemound Road
Milwaukee, WI 53213
Email: info@halleonard.com

In Europe, contact:
Hal Leonard Europe Limited
42 Wigmore Street
Marylebone, London, W1U 2RN
Email: info@halleonardeurope.com

In Australia, contact:
Hal Leonard Australia Pty. Ltd.
4 Lentara Court
Cheltenham, Victoria, 3192 Australia
Email: info@halleonard.com.au

WARMING UP

You love to sing. Most of the time your voice sounds pretty good, but every now and then you can't make it do what you want. Sometimes you can't get the high notes, or a fast run of notes sounds out of tune. Some songs sound better than others. What makes one day different from another, or one song different from another? There are a lot of factors that affect your voice: your physical health, your emotional well being, how much sleep you get, the weather, what you ate yesterday and, most of all, your skill. Your voice is built into your body, so you might not think of it as an instrument, but it is. You have to learn to play it, to keep it in shape and to house and feed it properly.

There are many skills involved in playing this instrument. Your pitch must be very accurate: every time you sing a note you should be right in the center of the pitch, not a little under it (flat) or a little above it (sharp). You shouldn't slide to the note (unless it's part of the style). Other elements of singing besides pitch are breathing, range, endurance, tone, volume, control, and stability. These can all be strengthened and improved by exercise. You also need to understand how to pick the right key for each song. There is a lot to learn in order to sing well night after night, without getting tired or hoarse. That's why voice lessons are so important. A good voice teacher will help you learn about every element of singing and help build the muscles you should be using and release the ones you shouldn't be using. As with anything physical, the better shape your muscles are in, the better you'll perform.

Since I am not watching you and listening to you sing, I can't give you a voice lesson, but I can get you started by giving you some basic exercises that will help get your voice warmed up. Before you start singing songs, you should stretch out the muscles of your instrument and gently remind them of the work they are about to do and how to do it properly. This is what a warm-up does.

Singing a song is not warming up. When you sing, you concentrate on how you sound and your body does whatever it takes to sound good. But that might not be the right thing to do. For example, you might try to get the high note by tightening your throat, but it will make your voice tired and possibly even damage your vocal cords. When you warm up, you isolate one problem at a time so you can focus on it and correct it. Warming-up will get your muscles stretched out and ready to sing.

USING THE AUDIO

This warm-up will give you an exercise for each area of your voice, but it isn't a substitute for voice lessons. If you are going to start taking your singing seriously, you will have to train just like a professional athlete does. This warm-up will get you off to a good start and will also give you an idea of what voice lessons are like. You should warm-up before any occasion when you will be singing: a rehearsal, a performance, a recording, and even before a voice lesson. If there are any exercises on this warm-up that make you feel tight or tired, don't do them; they aren't right for you.

There are two sets of warm-up exercises: twelve for women and twelve for men. Each exercise begins with an example of how it should sound. After the example, there is no singer, just the piano playing the exercise for you to sing. In one case, there are two examples at the beginning of the exercise because you are going to do it twice. Listen to the first example and run through the exercise doing it like the singer. Then go back, listen to the second example, and do it again the second way.

Some of these exercises might get too high or too low for you. If your throat feels tight, if you start straining or you can't hit the note, just stop and wait for the exercise to come into your range. After some work, you might be able to go higher or lower; but remember: everyone's range is different. You might be a tenor and not be able to reach the low notes of a baritone, or you might be an alto and not be able to go all the way to the top in the soprano range. That's fine. Develop your voice to its "personal best."

EXERCISE ONE

Warming Up Your Lower Voice

Sing this using the syllable "mah" (like the sound in "model").

We are starting with the voice that most people speak in. It's the lower part of your voice.

- Let your jaw drop
- Relax your shoulders
- Stop when it gets too high
- Join back in on the way down when it comes back into your range

One of the differences between speaking and singing is that when you speak you go right to the consonant at the end of the word. When you sing, you hold the vowels. That's what gives the sound its tone and pitch. That's why most exercises work on vowel sounds.

Women
Track 1

Men
Track 13

EXERCISE TWO

Warming Up Your Upper Voice
Sing this using the syllable "oo" (like the sound in "zoo").

You have two voices. We've already had an exercise for the lower one. This is for the upper one. Men, you are going to experiment with going into falsetto. Women, think like a soprano.

Your upper voice requires a bit more space inside your mouth in order to make a good sound, so as you sing this "oo" you are going to lift the roof of your mouth in the back (called the "soft palette"). It feels a little bit like yawning. Try to make this sound "hooty," like an owl.

After you feel comfortable doing this exercise on "oo," you can try it on "ee" and then on "ah" (which may be the hardest). Be sure to stay in your upper voice.

- Relax your shoulders
- Lift the roof of your mouth in the back
- Sing "oo"
- Stop if you feel like you're straining
- Drop out when the range becomes uncomfortable; come in again on the way back

Your voice is an acoustic instrument, which means it's like a hollow-body guitar or a piano rather than an electric guitar or a synthesizer. The sound goes into the body of the guitar, swirls around in all that lovely wood and comes out sounding rich and beautiful. The same is true for your voice. It swirls around inside your body before it comes out sounding like you. In your lower voice it swirls inside your chest and so it's called "chest voice." The higher voice is called "head voice" and it resonates inside your head. Your chest voice feels earthier, warmer, and has more bass in it; your head voice feels lighter, sweeter, and has more treble.

Women
Track 2

Men
Track 14

4

EXERCISE THREE

Connecting the Two Voices

Sing this using the syllable "wee" (like the sound in "week").

The top note of this exercise should be in your head voice and the bottom note should be in your chest voice. It takes some time before this exercise sounds smooth, so be patient. Don't try to push into your chest voice too early. Let it happen naturally.

- Relax your shoulders
- Lift the roof of your mouth for the top note
- Let your head voice cross gently to chest voice on the bottom
- Stop if you feel like you're straining
- Drop out when the range becomes uncomfortable; come in again on the way back down

It is not unusual to feel a "break" or a "crack" as you cross over from one voice to the other. Some people call it a "flip." This will smooth itself out over time if you don't try to force it. Let your chest voice come in when it's ready. Don't push to get it to come in sooner.

Women
Track 3

Men
Track 15

EXERCISE FOUR

Connecting in Both Directions, Pitch, Flexibility
Sing this using the syllable "ee" (like the sound in "tea").

As in the previous exercise, the top is in head voice and the bottom is in chest voice, but now you have to come back up to head voice again. This is usually harder. Try not to push your chest voice up too far. Let it go over easily into head voice. Also, pay attention to pitch: because the exercise is faster, the pitches are harder to hit accurately.

- Lift the roof of your mouth for the top note
- Let your head voice cross gently to chest voice on the bottom
- Lift the roof of your mouth as you go back up
- End at the top in head voice
- Stop if you feel like you're straining
- Drop out when the range becomes uncomfortable; come in again as it comes back into your range

The first note and the last note are the same, but it's hard to get them to feel the same. The first note is easier because you can lift the roof of your mouth as you inhale before you start singing. For the last note to feel as open, you must lift the roof of your mouth as you are coming back up the scale, before you get to the top note.

Women
Track 4

Men
Track 16

6

EXERCISE FIVE

Stabilizing the Tone

Five vowels on one pitch
Sing this using the syllables "oo, ee, oh, ah, eh" (like the sounds in "two, tea, toe, top, test").

Keep the pitch, the tone, and the volume exactly the same for all five vowels. The pitch is the actual note you are singing, how high or low it is. The tone is the sound of your voice. Does it get breathy or raspy? Does it move around? Does the sound change? It should stay solid and strong. When you sing songs, you create the tone and the pitch by holding the vowels. You may find that some of these vowels are weaker than others and that they shift as you get higher. They need to build in strength so that they are even all over your range.

- Keep the pitch constant
- Keep the sound of your voice the same as you move from vowel to vowel
- This should feel like one long line of sound that doesn't change except for the vowels
- Stop if you feel like you're straining

Women
Track 5

Men
Track 17

7

EXERCISE SIX

Loosening the Throat, Placing the Sound Forward
Sing this using the syllable "mm" (like humming).

A lot of people sing in their throat, which makes the voice get tired quickly. The solution is to put the sound further forward into your mouth. This exercise puts the sound as far forward on your face as possible: in your nose. It is a great warm-up, but you don't want to sing songs with the sound in your nose. Then it would have a nasal sound, which isn't pretty.

- Feel the sound in the bridge of your nose
- Go to head voice on the top notes
- Relax your jaw
- All of the air should be in your nose, not in your mouth
- Stop if you feel like you're straining

Women
Track 6

Men
Track 18

EXERCISE SEVEN

Loosening the Throat, Relaxing the Tongue
Sing this using the syllable "ghee" (like the sound in "geese").

The notes to this exercise are the same as the previous one except three times in a row. You might find this very challenging (which means it's really important that you do it!). If your throat gets tight when you sing, it will be hard for you to say the hard "g." Doing this exercise will teach those muscles not to squeeze and will help you learn to relax your throat while you sing. After a while, your tongue will start to feel sluggish and thick. Try to keep going anyway. It will loosen up eventually

- Go to head voice on top
- Say "ghee," not "kee"
- Be sure to get the top pitch; it's easy to go flat on this exercise
- Don't try to sing too much in chest voice; let it go to head voice
- Stop if you feel like you're straining

> If this exercise is difficult, it is because you are closing your throat when you sing. Closing your throat can help you find the pitch and produce a loud, strong sound, but it's very tiring and can make you hoarse. It can damage your voice. The basic premise of proper singing is that there is a direct connection between the air and the sound; none of the little muscles in your throat, neck, head, chest or jaw should tighten to get in the way. It's just air and sound.

Women
Track 7

Men
Track 19

EXERCISE EIGHT

Octaves: Pitch and Flexibility

Sing this using the syllables "oh, oo, oh" (like the sounds in "toast, two, toast").

Octaves are hard because they are so far apart. Jumping to a note is much harder than gradually walking up to it. In this case, the bottom note should always be in your chest voice and the top one should be in head voice. Besides all these things to think about, you also have to give less air pressure to the bottom note or it will "flip" when you move. Try giving it too much air pressure and you'll see what I mean. The bottom takes less air pressure and the top takes a bit more.

- Use head voice on the top note
- Lift the roof of your mouth for the top note
- On the bottom note, the roof of your mouth should be normal
- Keep the vowels "oh, oo, oh"
- Use less air pressure on the bottom note
- Stop if you feel like you're straining

> Once you get good at this one, try changing the top vowel. "Oo" is the easiest. Try "ee" or "ah." They are harder. Keep everything else the same: less air pressure on the bottom, lift on the top.

Women
Track [8]

Men
Track [20]

EXERCISE NINE

Flexibility, Pitch

Sing this using the syllable "nee" (like the sound in "neat").

This is a little complicated to learn, but it makes your voice feel so free that it's worth it. Learn it first on "nee" and then start doing the exercise on rolling tongue (rolled "r," like an Italian).

- Keep your face and lips relaxed
- Use head voice on the top note
- Come back to chest voice at the bottom
- Stop if you feel like you're straining

Women
Track 9

Men
Track 21

EXERCISE TEN

Flexibility, Pitch, Vocal Freedom

Sing this using rolling tongue (like an Italian) followed by "ee" (like the sound in "week").
Sing this using bubble lips (like a horse) followed by "oo" (like the sound in "zoo").

This exercise has two examples at the beginning. Do the rolling tongue version first, if you can. Then come back to the second example and do the bubble lips version.

The notes for this are the same as the last exercise, but you change sounds in the middle. Start with rolling your tongue and then switch halfway through to the "ee" vowel. The jumps in this exercise will improve your pitch and your flexibility (your ability to move rapidly from one note to another). Since the jumps are hard to do, you might be tempted to tighten your throat to give yourself some additional help. Of course we don't want you to tighten your throat, and that's where the rolling tongue helps. It keeps you from tightening. After the rolling tongue frees your throat, you switch to the "ee" vowel and try to keep the sensation of freedom.

This exercise goes back and forth between chest voice and head voice. Don't force it. Let it happen naturally. It will do it all by itself if you let it.

- Use head voice on the top note
- Come back to chest voice at the bottom
- The "ee" should feel as free as the rolling tongue
- The "oo" should feel as free as the bubble lips
- Keep your jaw relaxed
- Stop if you feel like you're straining

There are many singers who use their jaw muscles when they sing to help them control the sound. This is very tiring and can make you hoarse, so another way to go through this exercise is to sing the first half of the pattern on bubble lips and then switch to "oo." (Listen to the audio example to get the sound.) It helps if you put one finger on either side of your mouth just below the corners of your lips and lift your cheeks. This exercise will loosen your jaw, allowing you to sing the "oo" section freely.

Women
Track 10

Men
Track 22

EXERCISE ELEVEN

Range, Connection
The Waterfall
Sing this using the syllable "oo" (like the sound in "two").

There is no piano part for this exercise; the demonstration is just the singer singing two examples. This is an easy and fun exercise that you can do anywhere. Start at the top of your range in head voice and slide down through all the notes without stopping until you get to the bottom in chest voice. After you do it a few times going down, repeat it going up. Start on the bottom in chest voice and slide up into head voice. This might be harder. Think about making it sound lighter as you get higher. Also, if you lift the roof of your mouth in the back as you go up, it will help you to get across. As you work on it, the spot in the middle that feels like a "flip" or a "break" will start to smooth out.

> The easiest vowel to use for this exercise is "oo." Once you feel it getting smoother, try "ee" and then "oh."

Women
Track 11

Men
Track 23

EXERCISE TWELVE

Breath Control & Volume Control
Sing this using the syllable "ha."

When you sing, the air passes through your vocal cords and makes them vibrate. Controlling the air is a very important part of learning to sing. You may have noticed that singing quietly is very hard. Medium loud is the easiest and that is how you should sing most of these exercises. Loud is harder, and quiet is the very hardest. On this exercise, the "ha" sounds should be as short and as quiet as possible: tiny sounds. As you do this exercise and start to get tired, the sounds will get longer and louder. When you notice that this is happening, correct them by making them very short and quiet again.

- Use head voice on the top notes
- Come back to chest voice at the bottom
- Keep your jaw down and relaxed
- The sounds should be quiet and short
- Try not to let air escape between notes
- Stop if it gets too high

> Short notes are called "staccato." Smooth connected notes are called "legato." In this exercise the notes should be "staccato," quick and precise.

Women
Track 12

Men
Track 24

That's it! Now you are ready to sing. Pick a song that is comfortable for you. Try to apply what you have been working on in the exercises to the song. Relax your shoulders, open your mouth and let the sound come out. If you run into a problem spot, try to think about the exercise that seems to relate to it. Is the note high? Maybe it needs to go into your head voice. Or maybe the key should be lowered. Not everyone sings in the same key. If you gave the same song to two different singers, even if they were both very good, they would probably sing it in different keys.

Every voice is different, and your job is to learn everything you can about yours. That's a big assignment, but it's fun. Enjoy it and keep singing!

Lis Lewis is a voice teacher in Los Angeles, California. She is the author of *The Singer's First Aid Kit* (published by Creative Concepts, distributed by Hal Leonard Corporation) and director of The Singers' Workshop (*http://www.TheSingersWorkshop.com*), a website containing news, information, chat, products and classified ads for singers. She has been a voice teacher and performance coach for over twenty-five years, twenty of those years in Los Angeles. In addition to working with singers, she has worked in collaboration with managers, record labels, producers, and songwriters to get the best performances from their artists.

As a vocal coach, vocal producer, and a singer/songwriter Lis has worked with many remarkable people, some of whom are:

- Britney Spears, Herbie Hancock, Bobby McFerrin, Gwen Stefani (No Doubt), Jack Black, eastmountainsouth, No Secrets, Rus Martin (Hot Wire), Michel'le, Syreeta Wright, Richard Elliott, Lowen & Navarro and Mark Beeson
- the producers of Aretha Franklin, Whitney Houston, Mariah Carey, The Mamas & The Papas, The Pointer Sisters
- band members in Linkin Park, Dave Navarro's band, Alanis Morrisette's band, The Robert Cray Band, Trapt, The Don Henley Band, Kathy Matea's band, Journey, the 'E' St. Band, and Juliana Theory
- writers for Backstreet Boys, Bonnie Raitt, Pat Benatar, The Bangles, The Oak Ridge Boys, and The Miracles

Her own training started as a child at the world-famous Dalcroze School of Music in New York City as well as with private music teachers. She attended the University of Wisconsin at Madison and the University of Nebraska at Lincoln and has a Masters Degree in Theater and Music. She has taken post-graduate classes in music management, publicity, and marketing, as well as ongoing music training.

As a visiting lecturer or as an artist-in-residence, she has taught at colleges, music conferences, and music schools, including:

- Paul McCartney's Liverpool Institute of the Performing Arts, Liverpool, England
- EAT'M Music Conference, Las Vegas, Nevada
- Taxi Road Rally, Los Angeles, CA
- The Songwriter's Expo, Los Angeles, CA
- Singing For A Living, Los Angeles, CA
- Musician's Institute, Los Angeles, CA
- University of California Extension at Berkeley, CA
- UCLA Extension, Los Angeles, CA
- Santa Monica College, Santa Monica, CA
- National Academy of Songwriters, Los Angeles, CA
- The Blue Bear School of Music, San Francisco, CA

Lis can be reached at:

The Singers' Workshop
http://www.TheSingersWorkshop.com
lis@thesingersworkshop.com